THERE WILL BE BREAD AND LOVE

Books by

Robert P. Tristram Coffin

POEMS
>CHRISTCHURCH
>DEW AND BRONZE
>GOLDEN FALCON
>THE YOKE OF THUNDER
>BALLADS OF SQUARE-TOED AMERICANS
>STRANGE HOLINESS
>SALTWATER FARM
>MAINE BALLADS
>COLLECTED POEMS
>THERE WILL BE BREAD AND LOVE

ESSAYS
>BOOK OF CROWNS AND COTTAGES
>AN ATTIC ROOM

LECTURES
>NEW POETRY OF NEW ENGLAND
> *(Frost and Robinson)*

BIOGRAPHIES
>LAUD: STORM CENTER OF STUART ENGLAND
>THE DUKES OF BUCKINGHAM
>PORTRAIT OF AN AMERICAN
>CAPTAIN ABBY AND CAPTAIN JOHN

AUTOBIOGRAPHY
>LOST PARADISE

NOVELS
>RED SKY IN THE MORNING
>JOHN DAWN
>THOMAS-THOMAS-ANCIL-THOMAS

HISTORY
>KENNEBEC: CRADLE OF AMERICANS

TEXT
>A BOOK OF SEVENTEENTH-CENTURY PROSE
> *(With A. M. Witherspoon)*

There Will Be Bread and Love

By

ROBERT P. TRISTRAM COFFIN

NEW YORK, 1942

THE MACMILLAN COMPANY

ACKNOWLEDGMENTS

I am grateful to these periodicals for permission to include in this book poems which first appeared in their pages: *American Girl, American Mercury, Atlantic, Bowdoin Quill, Christian Science Monitor, Commonweal, Coronet, Extension Magazine, Forum, Free World, Good House-keeping, Harper's Magazine, Ladies' Home Journal, Lyric, New York Times, New Yorker, Old Farmer's Almanac, National Parent-Teacher, Saturday Review of Literature, St. Nicholas, Tuftonian, Virginia Quarterly Review.*

CONTENTS

[x]

THERE WILL BE BREAD AND LOVE

THERE WILL BE BREAD AND LOVE

I, Tristram, since my life roots deep in pain
Like ancient Tristram's, have the right again
To say the final things, and say them plain,
Being a poet. And I say them now.

I say you people have the right to trust
In certain things that will be, when our wars
Are over, or within them, if they last:
Water, I say, is one. There will always be
Blue water through the branches of some tree
And water high up as a wall behind some houses
And white sails going up, water by roads,
And maybe beasts will drink it under their loads,
Water in forests, and thin deer will drink it,
Or birds will dip it up drop after drop,
Too feverishly beautiful to stop,
Lifting bright beaks to thank whoever made it.
I say there will be hills, and trees will climb them
Gripping the rock with strong and knowing roots,
There will be hills with white clouds, and some fruits.
There will be cows to milk because it is evening
And they were lately big and bland with young,
New calves will totter under a rough tongue,
There will be milk for lambs and colts and others,
There will be fires lit and some songs sung.
Maybe the shapes of houses, cities, classes,
Vehicles, and laws will somewhat change,
But tools will not and mothers leaning to babies,
Giving the breast to them, will never seem strange.
No man's hand will ever be too bony,

[1]

Too cold from killing his own kind to take
A small son's hand in it and warm its fingers,
And when a strong man dies, some hearts will ache.
Always there will be some shapes like plows
Opening up furrows, sons got, hay in mows.
I do not think we ever shall finish with trees
Or have enough of honey, lambs, or bees.
I think a brother will be harder, tenderer
On a brother than on other men
And, being so, maybe will have wisdom
To be a brother to some nine or ten
Men who have a different man for father.
I think, too, that young men always will rather
Be with girls than with their kind in May.
There will be bread and love. These things, I say.

LATE CHRISTMAS

He filled the lantern, lit the wick,
It was so still he heard the tick
Of the small death-watch in the wall,
It didn't seem Christmas Eve at all.
The house was empty as a shell,
His grown-up sons had turned out well
And gone for good. Their mother lay
Outdoors now by night and day.
He took the lantern, got his pail,
Took his coat down from its nail,
And went out through the frosty shed.
Christmas was gone clean out of his head,
It was one milking time the more.
The milking stool was by the door.

He swung the door and raised his light,
And entered the midst of Christmas night:
Four damp legs and two big eyes
Tottered to meet him, friendly-wise,
Between the eyes as soft as silk
There was a star as white as milk
On the new young being there
Standing and staring its first stare.
A cow had been ahead of the mark,
Had come to her time there in the dark.
The man put down his light and knelt,
It might have been a child he felt,
The hair on the thin thing was so fine
To feel of in the lantern's shine.

[3]

THERE IS TOO MUCH TO A POET

A poet, it is plain to see,
Is a man of excess energy.

He has too many secret joys
To use up in begetting boys,
He has too much of hawk and fox
In him to set free in talks.

So he hides and has delight
Making new days deep in the night,
Running over hunger, trouble,
Living ahead, and living double.

His wife may think she has him all,
But he is running down the wall,
Burrowing where no mole can follow,
Climbing past the highest swallow.

Now he pulls out some bright thing
From his side, finds it a wing,
And he is off to gather honey,
Dark-tasting, brighter than new money.

He is too much a man to be
In one bed entirely,
So off he goes to climb his new
Beds and lie there two and two.

He is too full of leaning life
To stay a man, he turns a wife
And worships his own strength outside,
Being both bridegroom and the bride.

There is too much of him to stay
In a man, he runs away
Into the many boys that he
Was once and will hereafter be.

Creep upon him, seize his hair,
And you will have a lizard there,
Bright and quick, and he will escape
In many another lovely shape.

Before you have him caught and fast,
He will turn raindrops and go past,
He will be gone before you can
Say what he is, say he is man.

Think to hold him as a child,
He is a hairy man and wild,
And when you think to clasp his knees,
He is a rainbow over the trees.

YOUNG FARMERS

The man and woman walking there were young,
They held each other by the hand and swung
Their joined hands over their mounded garden row
Where sprouting beans were starting in to show.

It was as if these beans were all there was
To the universe, as if the laws
Of Spring had waited all these years to strew
These dots of green between these loving two.

Their first-born beans broke through the crumbling loam
Like crooked-up fingers, like the ones at home
Where the first son of this man and wife
Slept with month-old fists gripped full of life.

They could hold in no more, this wife and man,
With hands still clasped, they quickened step and ran,
Ran like the children they were yesterday
When school was out and they were bound for play.

A sixty-year-old farmer riding by
Saw the couple running, and his eye
Filled up with fire as an eagle's might
High in the sunset over coming night.

A GIRL SHELLING PEAS

Her slim white fingers run along the pod,
The secret spring lets go, and seven pearls
Loom suddenly set handsome in a row,
She will be woman, but just now a girl's
Slimness and stark certainty are in her,
She turns the peas out cool and fresh for dinner.

The peas fall in the pan with tender sound,
Only last night the first man's arm went round
Her slender waist resilient as the peas,
She was not sure she liked it. Her quick hands
Keep the green pearls falling between her knees,
The peas take iridescence one from other,
She will be kissed again, and be a mother.

The pods fly down like long-winged butterflies,
The pearls between her slim knees rise and glow,
Her dish fills swiftly. She is sweet and cool,
Just last night her lover told her so.
There will be many nights and his voice telling
Such things again, and many peas for shelling.

THE CRY

The night was too immense for any lantern,
Yet one was coming swinging down the road,
And someone's frosty breath was hung above it
And looked like dust of stars as someone strode.
There was no house for miles round any way,
But a light was coming on and life above,
Some woman or some man was in a hurry
On business like great worry or great love.
All at once, the lantern stopped in space,
Then rose, and lighted up an old man's face.

An old man's face did not belong out there,
It was too late and much too far to go,
The light did nothing to the deep-set eyes,
But it made the hair light up like snow,
It showed the dark fir trees and made them seem
Taller than common fir trees by the way,
It made the man all face without a body
And different from any man by day.
It hung there still, the quiet lonely light,
And it became the center of the night.

"Come back! It's all right now." The thin words were
Swallowed up and lost as a child's might be
When a child stops suddenly on a beach
And shouts against the whole mass of the sea.
"Come back, come back!" And nothing answered back,
The whole vast night drew back and still as death,
The only living thing in all that silence
Was the frosty cloud of old man's breath.
It was enough to make a whole night haunted
To hear that cry and not know who was wanted.

BUCK, BOY, AND TROUT

The boy slipped through the hazel woods so light
The trout poised in wet crystal took no fright,
Only a little clothing shut him in
From being free and slippery as his kin,
And no tattered shirt, no trousers hid
The beautiful cool things his body did.
He took his place, rooted in unstirred grass
And let the ripples of leaves and sunlight pass
Over him as over the water under,
His eyes were wide with shade and steady wonder,
He looked at the trout hung halfway there between
Air and earth. The water cut them clean,
The spots on them were like the freckles spread
On the boy's face, coppery, wild, and red,
The slender fish with rainbows at each fin
Were one piece with the boy's quick eyes and skin.

The boy let down his hook along a beam
Of shadow slanting down across the stream.

Ten yards above, without a rustled twig,
A buck-deer came out sudden, and his big
Eyes took in the boy and dancing brook,
The coppery spots along his slim ribs shook
As he breathed fierce and quiet seeing a creature
So like himself in every curve and feature,
He drank the stranger in so of his kind,
And through the sun-shot regions of his mind,
So like the brook, his hate flowed fast away.

Buck, boy, and trout stood slim in the flowing day.

[9]

It was one of the instants when there might
Be something more in common than the light
Through the universe. But the boy's eyes
Were sadder than the others', being wise
Enough to know, this young, the boy was doomed
To lose this instant the instant that it bloomed.

A little rainbow spread its wings and struck,
And there was trembling grass but never a buck.

THE MAY BASKET

The boy's ten fingers were as sore as soldiers,
He had no sisters, and he'd had to curl
The streamers of the white and rosy tissue
With scissor blades like ringlets on a girl.
He had to keep it secret from his mother,
But he had his first May basket done,
He'd braided horses' manes, the handle was easy,
His basket was a dream-lit cascade one.

The afternoon of agony with scissors
And fragile paper, paste, and lining, though,
Seemed like a sun fleck on the running water
Beside the time when day began to go.
A thousand hostile frogs had come out brazen
And shouted at the last stars April had,
The night had turned a month back into Winter,
The house he crept up to loomed wide and sad.

He took a quarter of his lifetime reaching
The doorstone and another quarter more,
With hammers striking each side of his forehead,
Before he hung the white thing on the door,
Where oftener the dark festoons were proper.
He felt the flush and agony of man,
He recalled too late the missing gumdrops,
Let the knocker fall, and shrank, and ran.

He ran as never rabbit ran the hillside,
His bent knees changed his height to suit each ledge,
Took juniper or bayberry, swords or daggers,

He did not stop until the swamp's dark edge,
He squatted with the frogs in their wet alders,
Listened, but only heard his heart's own stress.
If she became the mother of his children,
She would have to do it all by guess.

SPRING, SPRING, SPRING

Now days are days of new blue weather,
Peepers and plowmen out together.

The smallest brook begins to boil,
The farmers begin to smell of soil.

They spill their farms off in their rooms,
Their women sweep it out with brooms.

Roosters blush along their hackles,
Henpens turn to mountains of cackles.

White clouds catch on every tree,
Lambs leap on legs without a knee.

Lambs and clouds leave tufts of wool
On everything. Rain-barrel's full.

Life runs sparkling from the eaves,
Flowers come before the leaves.

Rhodora blossoms out of bark,
The shadbush shines long after dark.

The bluets ice the fields like cakes,
Hills spill long jewels of the snakes.

Round men sow the corn in rows,
Flat men stand and scare the crows.

The crows are puzzled by white twine,
And they discuss it on a pine.

The frogs have sown the pools with seeds,
And future tadpoles float in beads.

Night's peepers have so much to say
They overflow into the day.

They cannot stop for anything
But shout it over, "Spring, Spring, Spring!"

A FLICKER WENT FREE

The youngest boy of three climbed down the stairway
In the house gone perilous with dark,
He was but one step ahead of dreaming,
Dreams whispered after him, he did not hark.

He had to do it while his brothers were sleeping,
He found the cage and felt along the wire,
Put in his quivering hand and felt the tremble
Of the bird built out of trembling fire.

The wild thing did not flutter, for the terror
Of a starless world had numbed its soul,
It lay gentle in the boy's thin fingers,
A handful of the wind in a soft roll.

It was a floating tissue of creation
No heavy thing such as a hand should clutch,
A flicker, with the secret fire waiting
Under its wings for the spark of flight to touch.

The boy went to the door and drew it open,
A waning moon of May hung in the sky,
It drenched the captive flicker's beak with silver
And lit a minute star in either eye.

The whole night caught its breath in, and it waited,
The slim moon lifted up the wild bright tips
Of its ears, no breath came through the hollow
Between the youngest boy's wide-open lips.

[15]

The boy uncurled his hand, the spotted flicker,
With a moon scrolled on its head and throat,
Moved no more than the incredible petals
Where the white wild water-lilies float.

Then the boy sobbed deep, the feathers rankled,
The airy feathers tautened into air—
The bird was gone, the sound of a loosened bowstring,
Wildness, and a boy alone were there.

MAINLAND-WOMAN'S RETURN

The bay was full of sparks of Autumn light,
Fair-weather waves ran turning over white.
The island was too lonesome for a wife
Used to wanting people in her life.

No man could ask for any finer day
To take his wife home to her folks for a stay
That, from the looks of things, would turn out one
Not measured by a moon or by a sun.

She was going in her husband's boat,
It was the handsomest reach-boat afloat—
High in the nose, gold stripe upon the black—
The man stood lonely steering at the back.

Behind him came two other boats filled low
With people sitting quiet in a row,
The women had on hats, the men kept eyes
On the place where sea's blue met the sky's.

The engines throbbed. The front man did not turn
Once to look at anything astern,
He kept his eyes towards mainland and far trees
And the narrow cargo at his knees.

Autumn leaves had heaped the cargo higher,
The man stood over two hues of lovely fire
Burning on the box with silver grips,
And steered his boat with sunlight on his lips.

THIS WAS THE WORD

Neither he nor the others had to speak,
They all knew the man had come out on a peak
Of his life, and was a poet crowned.
The woman handed him the nicked and browned
Breadboard, and she said, "You cut the bread.
This is the board where Sidney Lanier once
Cut the loaves of bread for all his sons."
He took the loaf and knife and went ahead.

His hands trembled, for this he was doing now
Was something like a man's taking the plow
Or taking over the seed-bag from his father
In the Spring of the year when a man would rather
Sow the corn than eat. This was warm fact,
This was hard seeds, a putting of hands in earth,
Shaping something capable of birth,
This was a certain, sacrificial act.

The man pressed down the worn bright knife
And cut straight lines, the lines of life
Along, across the others there in wood
Cut by the poet who had understood
The common tongue of water, bread, and bird.
The carver opened the white flesh of the wheat
And gave it to the hungry ones to eat,
This was the word, the quiet holy word.

NEW ENGLANDERS ARE MAPLES

New Englanders are like the pasture slopes
Behind their barns. You put them down as sober,
And then one day you wake up, and you find them
Red and golden maples of October.

It takes adversity or coming close
To trouble and hard times to make them glow,
Then they really flower as swamp maples
Flower on the edge of frost and snow.

You might suppose that they were never going
To be much more than middling fair to good,
When suddenly they are new people wholly,
Burning bushes blazing in the wood.

Maybe they had such hard time getting born,
What with the cold and all, they feel they must
Be born again, and so in age and trial
They blossom out of death and out of dust.

They are good people for your nearest neighbors
When the deep old earth's foundation slips,
It is good to have behind the barn
The flame and beauty of the Apocalypse.

APPLE-JORDAN

Apple-Jordan was the last
Of his family. All had passed
Over the edge before they went
And talked a steady low talk meant
For other ears than ears of neighbors
As they went about their labors.
None of the men had ever married.
Now Apple-Jordan kept and carried
On the farm his brothers left.
There was no more to him in heft
Than there was to a boy thirteen
Running the hills and keeping lean.

And something in the Jordan place
Had touched old Apple in the face,
And his eyes smiled at secrets known
To Apple and to him alone,
His eyes were always on men's knees,
Apple's talk was like the bees
In swarming season as he hoed
Alone, or milked his cows or mowed.
He always ran from this to that,
The women all were frightened at
Apple in woods or in the clear,
But he was harmless as a deer.

Yet there was one thing Apple could
Do better than any man who stood
Above the ground, and that was graft
Apple trees. The men who laughed

And used the nickname on the queer
Fellow were glad that he lived near,
For he could take a native tree,
Sour as this world can be—
A seedling coming down somehow
From the Indians, sown by a cow
In a pasture—and make it bring
Forth full-moon apples of Governor King.

This man could make the wild wood tame,
His eyes would light up like a flame
As he notched the greening bark
And set the shoot in so the spark
Of life that shot up through the rind
Of the wild branch there would find
The new vein so exquisitely placed
That the urgent new life raced
Up to tame buds, two or three,
Which would become a whole new tree,
And hard small apples hung below
Would blush to see huge apples glow.

Apple would come to graft as soon
As it was time to by the moon,
He would not hurry, he had his reasons,
He kept the proper times and seasons,
The moon must be a waxing one
When good grafting could be done.
But best of all times was in March
When the full moon raised its arch
Of golden fire through bare trees;
Then men saw Apple on his knees

At work and with a thousand friends
To talk to at the world's dark ends.

Apple-Jordan, wryly crotched,
Set the grafts in where he had notched
The severed limb, each side the cut;
He bent and panted, lean of butt,
Made his knife flash like the lightning.
For years thereafter all the whitening
Orchards full of bees and life
Declared, as plainly as a wife
With children round her, pink and stout,
That a man had been about
His handsome work and left his mark
White and clear against the dark.

UNGATHERED GRAPES

The bunch of grapes my pickers did not find
Hangs here with Autumn moonlight on its rind;
The color that hid it well from thrifty eyes
Betrays it to the moon a larger size.

It shall hang there safe for all of me,
It would be wrong to touch what seems to be
A free-will offering, though made against the grain,
To brief northern sunshine and the rain.

I wonder who will win this bag of booty
When frost will thin these leaves and bare its beauty?
Maybe the crow in glossy Winter cloak
Who comes to call when chimneys do not smoke.

Or it may be that master-thief, the jay,
The curious, nervous squirrel, red or gray,
Or on a night of frost the sharp raccoon's
Frosty eyes may spy these clustered moons.

Or they may fall before the field-mouse's nose
Where he walks moonlight on his careful toes.
But whatsoever creature is the one,
These grapes will bring him back the Summer sun.

It is a lovely thought to leave behind:
These grapes that have the moonlight for their rind,
Fruit for the wild and not for lips of mine,
Mean more than all I harvested from the vine.

BED OF FIRE

One night was worth all of the rest,
And that was when he slept all dressed
With his father upon a ledge.
The cold March night had put an edge
On all the stars. But he had heat,
It came from the ledge, came upward sweet,
Sweetness of fire his father and he
Had kindled of juniper and bayberry.

Out on the pasture they cleared that day,
Where the fire had lain, they lay,
Two live things who made their bed
Of fire and felt the vast earth spread
Under them lovingly, glad to keep
Its arms around them in their sleep.
And the boy went drifting towards new dreams
With eyelids touched by stars' cold beams.

In the dreams the father grew
Wide as the world, and he had his two
Arms around all starry space,
The son looked his father in the face,
Saw his father was earth entire,
And saw the heart in him was fire,
Saw himself there snugly curled
Beside the beauty of the world.

MENNONITE FARMER

I met him driving on ahead of a shower,
He was dark center to the dazzling flower
Of the thunderhead. His face was square
As his carriage top, his hat, his hair.

What womenfolks he had stowed in behind
No one could see, for they were riding blind
In a carriage with no lights set in
To let the blinding sunlight through or sin.

The fields were whitening wheat each side the man,
The richness of the earth flowed out and ran
And met the sky each side the patriarch,
His face was bare and his hard mouth a mark.

He stared with bleak and barren innocence,
Behind his narrow head the cloud's immense
Whiteness changed to dark, a lightning crack
Ran down and split the rising world of black.

The man's eyes glistened as the sun went out,
He was a farmer, he did not know about
The hot and hidden fire set apart
In the teeming darkness of his heart.

He did not know that he had come this way
In an earlier and robust day
When men of tents and concubines and kine
Built God out of honey, milk, and wine.

He little knew what holy and rich sweet
Had beautified and hallowed his washed feet,
What power spread his narrow forehead broad.
But I knew, and I touched my hat to God.

THANK LITTLE BOYS

School is out, and little boys turn loud,
They come out pushing, and they stand up proud,
Their eyes blaze fire as they look for slights,
They double fists and stand up for their rights,
Perilous and ancient maleness grips them.
The bold boy seizes shyer boys and trips them,
He cannot help it, it is cut in stone
A thousand dead men built this law in bone.

Do not blame the boys, but blame us rather,
Blame every strong and loving father's father.
Go to the barnyard and see cockerels peck
And face each other with a bristling neck,
Tails in the air, and clash their spurs like knives.
Thank little boys who bear new precious lives
Through daggers and stings of bitter weathers on them
And hold their tails up with no feathers on them.

FRIEND FROM THE WORLD'S END

I thought the island was my own
And fancied I was sole alone,
I did not know what gentle eyes
Were watching all my privacies.

A gull went by, his white head turned,
And one dark eye upon me burned
For three beats of his wings or four,
Then did not see me any more.

But something told me I was being
Watched steadily by something seeing,
I knew I was, although my gaze
Was on the spire of my blaze.

So I turned towards the sea,
And two mild blue eyes looked at me,
And a silky head of jet
Lifted high as it could get.

It was a seal that wondered why
I had taken from the sky
Part of the sun and now saw fit
By his cool waves to play with it.

His body passed but not his two
Eyes, they stayed there steady blue,
I smiled at him, his eyes grew black,
I was sure the seal smiled back.

He humped and vanished without sound,
But there he was when I turned round,
And I was proud that from earth's ends
The seal had come up to make friends.

THE SPOON

Digging his cellar, they found a spoon
A hundred years old. The same old tune
Sung there once would be sung once more.
Who was he to think a door
Could shut him off from the old refrain?

Sleek-haired boys would run again
Who ran before his father ran,
No house held a single man,
Part of it was the vagrant dead,
Dead strangers kept small rooms in his head
And some days threw their windows wide
On bees that swam like a golden tide
In sunlight lost two centuries back.
Every so often there was a track
With two toes only instead of five.

The same old melody. Being alive
Was being an army of weary ones,
Keeping abreast of the moons and suns,
Coming up tall and going down,
Bled bone-white and burned earth-brown,
Meek and submissive yet never broken.

The words in his house would be words spoken
By ancient strangers who loved him not
But loved his strength and the sons he got.

CUT DIAMOND

The afternoon would be a scar forever
On the boy's bright mind. He saw the swoop,
And mighty wings came open, full of shadow,
Among the sunlit hens beside the stoop.

Then out of nothing but a cloud of feathers
The thing came clear, a monstrous bird, cut sharp,
Beating its wings and dwindling in the sky shine
And leaving sounds like strings snapped on a harp.

But something else there was, and that was terror:
The bird was double, there was another one
In below the hawk and headed with him
But wingless and head bowed towards the sun.

The upper bird was fastened in the lower
By hooks that bit into its quiet back
And made the lower wings dead walls of feathers,
The double bird went on its shining track.

And sounds came down from somewhere, shrill and lonely,
Cries no earthly creature ever cried,
Falling like sad bells and dwindling, dwindling,
The bird had dwindled out before they died.

Yet always this one watching now would hear them
And see the double bird shrink to a spark
And think of cruelty hardened to a diamond
Burning the world and bringing on the dark.

BRIDE OF THE SUN

The farmer's wife knew she was treading stars,
She went careful, making no rude jars,
And opened up her oven doors and saw
Her twin and browning tablets of the law.

She drew her twin loaves out, put down her ear
Close to their hot sweet plumpness, she could hear
Them singing to themselves a melody
They sang in common with the nebulae.

She put the loaves back in and let them sing
Their cosmic song out deep inside the ring
Of handsome flour, she well knew her place,
She would not meddle with the angels' grace.

She sat herself down in her rocking-chair
And gave her bread ten hot more minutes there,
Then she took it out, the song was done,
And she blushed like a young bride of the sun.

YOUNG SPRING

Where the hot rocks tumbled high
I came on a piece of fallen sky.

Filaments of moonstone froth,
Translucent, strange and lovely cloth.

It looked as if the west wind's breath
Would shatter it and be its death.

Azure links, an airy chain,
Told me Spring had come again.

A snake had crept out of his skin
And left it lying bubble-thin.

I went carefully down the hill,
Fearful of doing a bluet ill.

I walked light as if my legs
Moved among blue robin's eggs.

I went light as anything
For fear I might disturb young Spring.

THE APPRENTICE LOBSTERMAN

The room was cold, the fire was black out
In the barrel stove, but there was fire
In the big man bending the spruce bows
To heat him and the boy built out of wire.

The boy fed laths into the man's wide hands,
The man spat out bright nails between his hums
And drove them in with one hard hatchet blow,
It was so dark, his eyes were in his thumbs.

Outside the open door, the steel March sky
Had light still on it, and across the light
An arrow of dark geese slid fiercely north
And left wild sounds between the day and night.

The snow still showed in patches by the door,
With yellow signatures of the man and boy,
This was a house where women did not come
To sweep the shavings up or dull the joy.

The room was hung with rope and smelled of tar,
The thorny skeletons of lobster claws
Crackled there, the boy initiate
Was learning silence and the old male laws.

He held his breath and watched the lobster trap
Take shape, a house all windows and no door,
With windowy stairways fashioned to tempt in
The cold dark creatures on the ocean floor.

The boy would be a man tomorrow, so
He drank the man in deep, and every motion
Became a part of him, new suns would see
This grace and strength out swinging on the ocean.

SETTING HEN

She sets upon her nest. The sounds come in
Of hens that are as she was yesterday,
Her eyes grow wider, and they shine amazed,
Hearing frivolity a world away.

She has not moved a feather these four hours,
A prowling rat had taken her for dead
And nosed up closer, but he turned and ran
When he saw fire blaze each side her head.

She is so quiet every rustling straw,
Every unexplainable low stir
In dead dry wood has kept her head erect,
Plain sunbeams on the floor seem strange to her.

There are nine things below her hovering weight,
And they have grown to her, they are a part
Of her alertened being, and they have
The same warmth as the center of her heart.

Her small mind knows what thing is going on,
It is more consequence than food or fear,
She sits on her religion, and she dares
Rats, the sun, and silence to come near.

Anybody with good sight
Could tell this farm was good, all right.
There was a clam-rocker full of red
Astrachans by the flowerbed,
The red showed through the wooden slats.
Two worlds met here, and the cats
Would be plump and sleek, the nets
Would be spread on violets
And white clover blooms to dry.
This would be a place to lie
On bunched-up hay and smell the sea,
The bees would blend marsh-rosemary
With Queen Anne's lace in honey cells.
The flowerbed had white clamshells
Around it. Farming here was two
Kinds of work, and play all through;
Boys driving home the cows would meet
The long fogs coming, boys' hot feet,
At the end of every row,
Could be cooled in flakes of snow
Where the ocean curled in white,
This was a saltwater farm, all right.

A FARM

A farm is more than hives of bees
Or cows all feeding towards the breeze,
A farm is more than fields of stubble
And helping small lambs over trouble,
Weaning calves upon your fingers,
Mending carts while Winter lingers.

A farm is a mysterious place
Where you can come out face to face
With yourself at lonely labor,
A farm is making a good neighbor
Out of rain or wind or snow
And guiding life along the flow
Of the soil beside a plow,
Saving Summer in a mow.
A farm is where boys grow to men
When they are barefoot still and ten,
And men stay boys enough to see
Brothers in butterflies and the tree.

A farm is something like a wife,
Labor that adds up to life,
A farm is something you can trust
To build you children out of dust.

THE FIRST CHRISTMAS TREE

He felt he must be nearly man-grown now,
For they had sent him after the Christmas tree,
They had left it to him to decide
What a proper Christmas tree should be.

They trusted him to take the sharpest axe,
He carried it over his shoulder like a man,
It took a lot of balancing, for the thing
Was half as long as he was in its span.

He went as quiet as a man would go,
He surprised a squirrel into laughter,
And a partridge went up from a stump
And left a roll of sudden thunder after.

The first fir was too wide for any room,
The next was on a hillside, and the wind
Had blown it all one way, south side was good,
But the northern side of it was thinned.

He took his time. A tree outdoors looked small,
But when you got it in a room, it grew
Strangely taller, somehow, and its plume
Bent sidewise on the ceiling all askew.

A boy had eyes much bigger than his belly,
His father always said. He must take care
Not to be a boy. He found the right tree,
It was too lovely, though. He left it there.

He found one almost perfect at the last,
He walked three times around it to make sure,
He lopped the lower boughs off neat and even
And brought it down with two cuts to the core.

He took it at the balance, standing deep
With feathery boughs half smothering his face,
He walked in fragrance down the darkening hill,
The stars were coming out in deep blue space.

The brightest star of all just tipped his burden,
A man's strength rippled in his boyish thighs,
His breath was round him like the down of angels,
He walked in Christmas deep as his two eyes.

THIS WAS THE WAY THE WINDS WENT

I saw his face lit up as by the sun,
But it was a foggy day, and there was none,
The fisherman's face burned with his own life-blood,
His energy poured out in a red flood
Of licking flames that ate themselves up fast.
He stood and watched his fire as I passed :
Three hundred lobster traps, two Winters of work,
Lacework of slender wood turned into murk,
Arches of spruce and cobwebs of tarred twine
Funnelled to let dark lobsters in to dine
But never out again. The man stood there
Watching his life go back to earth and air.

The man had ceased to fight. It was too late.
The fire lit his face and showed the great
Seams the north and south wind had laid wide.
Anger and grief had gone, and only pride
Was left upon his forehead and hard chin.
This was not misfortune. This was not sin.
This was the way the winds went, this the weather,
Only a day, an hour, good things hung together,
A net of meshes of moments, the ruin came,
If not by teeth of ledges, then by teeth of flame.
But a man has many nets in him
Before he lies down old and cold and dim.

DUTY

He carried his water in a slippery jug,
Half the size that he was, in a hug,
He did not let his solemn blue eyes roam
But fixed them steady on the sight of home.

The trousers on him were no longer than
A drink of water for a thirsty man,
His heart was on a level with the white
Daisies tipping over, spilling light.

Butterflies went by, he did not follow,
Almost on his hair a skimming swallow
Snipped the pinions from a silvery moth
That might have taken yellow curls for cloth.

A gay procession of black ants marched by,
The boy did not so much as twinkle an eye,
He did not stop, he did not turn aside,
He staggered on turning his toes out wide.

It was the boy's first going to the spring
To get the drinking water, and no thing
On wings or legs, on earth or in the air,
Was going to keep him from his errand there.

This was the boy's first step away from play,
And his head was higher than the day,
His brief trousers in their heated span
Felt the first faint spark that would be man.

[42]

It was a greater joy than he had known
That day he took his foremost step alone,
He stumbled blindly on into new beauty
Brighter than all the butterflies, called duty.

JUSTICE

There is a justice outside courts we know,
I saw it in my barn and stood below.
A mother swallow and a father swallow
Came almost faster than my eyes could follow
Through the high window, never both together,
And so not able to tell each other whether
This young-one fed the last, or that or that,
And neither stopped to judge which crop looked fat,
But each shot in and fed the proper one,
The emptiest, and back out in the sun.

The wide bills opened at the selfsame angle,
The five necks rose from out the hairy tangle
In the nest the same height at the sound
Of wings that told the blind food was around;
It would have taken Solomon to say
Which bill was widest and hungriest that day,
And yet there never was a single miss.
One bird was there, bent down and gave the kiss
Of parenthood, was gone, and in its stead
The other came, a new wide mouth was fed.

Any man who saw it would confess
This was a lovely chain of righteousness.

NEW ENGLAND HILLSIDE

The night goes down the hill below
The birches, and the clear stars show
Where stones have fallen from the wall,
There is no wastefulness at all.
Lamplit houses line the deep
Valley down below, and sleep
Is coming into them house by house.
Not a whippoorwill, not a mouse
But knows his right place in this plan,
The balsam trees have learned from man
How to moderate their will
And make the most of a steep hill,
How to make the most of narrow
Life left after plow and harrow
Have taken their share and how to press
Into a small place loveliness.
Even the dead know, their cold bones
Are lying where too many stones
Would leave the corn roots little room,
Where only hardhack spikes can bloom.

The houses that are going dark
Shelter ones who toe the mark
Their ancestors learned how to toe
Among long harvests of the snow
And the short ones of the corn.
These old friends of stone and thorn
Are going to bed to save the light
And letting neat birches have the night.

CLOUDY SUNSET

A long hand came out from the westering sun
Under the clouds and fingered one by one
Dark islands half a leaden sea away,
And they came close and quivered with golden day.
A seagull caught afire on the dark
Ceiling of the world and went like a spark
Out over the waves and set the world afire,
A hill became bright houses and a spire,
A seaport turned white piles of children's blocks,
And they were precious stones that had been rocks—
Diamond dust was sprinkled on each tree,
And there were silver nets dragged on the sea.
A fisherman stood in his boat, his hips
Were suddenly bathed in the Apocalypse,
The mackerel net he was running clear of weeds
Became an endless cobweb hung with beads
Of a fiery morning which the man
Was pulling from the evening ocean's span.
The light moved over the water and the land.

A mysterious and a golden hand
Was counting out the jewels which men had
Believed were reefs and wharves and boats or sad
Houses where they lived on little light,
The hand was putting pearls away for night.

NEEDLES IN HAYSTACKS

Pins and needles of the frost,
Such bright and fine things soon are lost.

Who can find the sweet-grass blade
When the hay is stacked and made?

Who keeps account of the small words
Sung by wings of humming-birds?

Who keeps the humming-bird's slight young
In the airy nest she's swung?

Long winds never blow away
Birds as gossamer-light as they.

Great gales leave the spider's ladder,
Thin as the quick tongue of the adder.

Rain will spare the ants' pale eggs
And blue butterflies' thin legs.

Suns will wander from the mark,
Clash, and leave a universe dark.

But the humming-bird's very light
Young emerge out of the night,

Start the cyclones of their wings,
And join the safe and slender things.

FIVE BARE BOYS

Five young boys leap out of their pants,
They run in old male arrogance
Along the spring-board, and they dive,
Rampant, shining, as alive
In the air as on the ground,
Each makes an arc of treble sound
And vanishes in silver bubbles.
A bird sings low, there are no troubles
In all the world, the world stands still.

But up the boys come, and they spill
Water and laughter, arch their tails,
Five small hard and happy males,
They gleam naked, blare like horns,
Sharp and beautiful as thorns.
They drown the bird out, rankle white,
Five slender barbs of appetite,
And the universe can spin
On its handsome way again.

NEW ENGLAND CONSERVE

The grapes he was eating here were ones
Ripened and sweetened by the suns
That browned his bare feet as he ran
Ten Summers before he was a man.

Under his whitening hair he thought
How vast trees now grew on the spot
Where the vine which bore this fruit
Had once found honey with its root.

So his mother in her prime
Had won her victory over time,
Her aging sons would all confess
The worth of her New Englandness.

The life of far forgotten heat
Tasted still and tasted sweet,
This was what it meant to be
Dipping in immortality.

THE WARM SPOT IN THE PASTURE

The boy's bare feet were mostly toes and ankles,
His face was mainly freckles and sharp chin,
But his eyes were wide as handsome morning
When the morning star is growing thin.
His overalls cut him deep, for he was growing,
He carried pails so full he put a chip
Of clean white birch upon the morning's water
So the bulge of crystal would not drip.

The spring his father had walled in a barrel
Was two pinewoods and a pasture from the house,
The late September dew made chilly footing
For the barefoot boy, but there were cows
Getting up from sleeping in the pasture,
And they left places for a boy to pause,
Set his pails down there and do some thinking,
Get his breath and take what warmth there was.

When he got to a cow's place in the pasture,
He stood upon the dry spot with both feet,
And his eyes grew brighter blue and wider
As his cold feet soaked up last night's heat.
The steady warmth the cow had printed deeply
In the earth came up the boy's whole length,
He stood there still, and he outgrew his trousers
With good will and warmth and borrowed strength.

THE BONFIRES

Tremendous things had happened overnight,
The maple trees were new trees made of light,
Leaves no more, but clustered tongues of flame,
Outrageous fire that made the sun look tame.
The light came out of the maples. This was blood
Redder than a man's was, or a flood
Of golden fire no one guessed could be
Hidden in the coolness of a tree.

Here were trees no more but bonfires standing
Up along the earth, and their expanding
Radiance cast a glow on ground, on stones,
On grass, and lightened monotones
As fires light up faces in the dark.
After this, no one could say that bark
Of trees had only quiet under,
When trees one night could turn so into thunder.

THE POLES

Each child upon the glassy beach is two,
One child with his head up, one head down,
Running just as fast and just as true
And touching his bare toes on toes as brown.

The children's eyes are flakes blown off the sea,
The puffs of sudden foam and they are brothers,
They run as far as waves will let them be
Away from hands and voices of their mothers.

They pick up sugar cookies made of shell
With stars pricked finely on their upper crust,
The mothers and the fathers sit and look,
The children run and shout because they must.

They run and do not know where they are going,
Their elders mean no more than that white tower,
The lighthouse far at sea, white birds are snowing
As if someone had picked apart a flower.

Out on the headland where the wide gales lean
Minute daisies blossom sweet and mild,
These are the poles and all that is between,
The savage ocean playing with a child.

TWO WOMEN UNDER A MAPLE

I came around a corner of the day
Expecting to find more brown men making hay,
For haying time was at its highest tide
And men too busy to let the small boys ride,
The sun was up ten minutes of twelve o'clock,
It was no time for tales or love or talk.

And two wives cool as Summer wives can be
Were playing checkers under a maple tree,
They had white aprons on and sleeves rolled high
As if they had just left an apple pie,
Shade and sunlight polka-dotted their faces,
They moved their checkers with no airs or graces.
There they sat refuting, square of chin,
That resting is New England's cardinal sin.

THE WHISPERERS

My three pasture-pines stood tall
And quiet as the old stonewall
They grew out of in a row,
I thought I heard the grasses grow,
It was so still and fair a day
Above the pasture where I lay.

Then something happened over me,
And all at once I heard each tree
Give a sigh and then commence,
One after one, a low, intense
Whisper, though there was no breeze
I could see. The three old trees
Had something on their mind. Each one
Waited till his mate was done
And answered then, as plain as plain,
Each whisper rose and fell again.

I knew that they were talking together,
Perhaps it was a change of weather,
Nothing to me who have a house,
But life or death to bird or mouse,
Perhaps they knew the wind was coming,
And that set all their thin leaves humming
A myriad syllables as fine
As dust motes in a sunbeam's shine.

Whatever they said was like the sea.
And suddenly I knew 'twas me
The pines were whispering so about,
They were afraid I might find out

What they said, so they spoke low,
I heard their small words come and go
Like some language long forgot.
I listened hard, but I could not
Make it out, though all my head
Sang with loveliness they said.

KITCHEN SUN-DIAL

"The leg of mutton at the second crack,
The apple pie goes in at number seven"—
And the mother fixed her hat and went
And left her daughter at the gate of heaven.

This farm mother had no use for clocks;
She timed herself and life by older things:
The daybreak cock called time to light the fire,
Swallows cried supper with high-flying wings.

The window of the kitchen faced the south,
That was a clock for anyone to trust,
The sun marked minutes on the kitchen floor
As it slanted in aflame with dust.

Twenty minutes from this crack to that,
An angel cake was these two floor-boards wide,
The sun kept exquisite tally as it marched
Around the world and this farm's shining side.

Calm in the very center of her farm,
This woman with her hands in flour and heat
Measured life out to man and boys and girls
By sunlight, measured life out hot and sweet.

Three inches of white pine—a johnnycake,
Twelve inches of the floor—a chicken pie;
Laws of the Medes and Persians, squares of gold
That slid along the floor and did not lie.

The mother brought her girls up every one
By laws of sunlight. Now this youngest, last
Daughter knew her feet were at the gate,
She put the roast in, and her heart sang fast.

THE EXPEDITION

The moon was large, the boy was small. These two
Were out together at last, and no one with them.
The moon went low along the fence top with the boy,
And it kept looking at him every time
The trees got by or where the wall dipped low.
The boy had often thought of making friends
With the moon like this, and here he was.
When he stopped still, the moon stopped moving, too,
And looked at him, and he looked back at it.
After a little, though, he took to walking
Faster and faster, and things were not the same,
He wished the moon would look some other way.
He started to run. And then he came out bare
On a wide hill, and there the white moon was
Miles away and not with him at all,
There were woods and more woods in between
And water with another moon inside.

Suddenly the boy sat down and cried.
After a while, his father found him there.
He and the moon would never be friends again.

BAD WINDS BLOW SOME GOOD

A bad wind always plows some good:
The hurricane felled pines that stood
Against the clouds and levelled flat
Briars where rabbits sit down at
Their housekeeping and family duties,
And so those smooth and silky beauties
Who live on rabbit meat and wind,
Red foxes, read the breeze and grinned,
To think of all the domiciles
Open to them for miles and miles,
But the rabbits moved to town,
And I could see them sitting down
On my citified young beets
And flattening my lettuce with their seats,
So I went out and gave them grown
Carrots, to leave my carrots alone,
So now I have the forest grace
Tumbling bright-eyed around my place,
Forest silks and jewel eyes
And downy mischief every size—
And this I should not have at all
Without a hurricane to fall
Upon the woods and briar patches
And foxes pulling at the latches
Of rabbits' homes till rabbits flee
And come to town to live with me!

FAIR FEELING

When country families go downhill in town,
The feeling for a fair is last to go
Of all the substance of the loyalties
That made them handsome neighbors to the snow.
Quiet went the first, and loneliness
And shyness did not linger long behind;
Pride stayed on in living by the day,
But pride, for all its toughness, can go blind.

These lost ones have locked up the house and come
Out to the fair with no glance at the sky,
They have their best clothes on, but do not smile,
They drift where crowds stand thick to stare or buy.

But now and then, one of the lost will halt
Where a shelf of jellies stains the sun
And wonder why he thinks of a boyhood church
And does not know he is in an older one
Than that his boyhood knew, one with old glass,
One lighted by the ancient color of man.
Another stares at pumpkins worshipping
Gods older than those gods whose altars ran
With golden fire in Baalbek or Babylon;
He thinks of an Autumn woodland he once saw,
And bows his head a moment, and is gone.
And one lost one will pause where cattle stand
With wide eyes rolling full of fear and light,
He drops his eyes unwilling to meet theirs,
And he will dream of sunflowers tonight.

THE GOSLINGS

The boy was in the middle of a dream—
And being seven, his dream was full of sun—
When the sounds awakened him, and he
Woke into an even brighter one.

From his high bed he saw into the kitchen,
His father was down kneeling by the door,
His mother was on her knees there, too, beside him,
They had the lamp down with them on the floor.

Their shadows were high up along the ceiling,
They seemed half strangers and a bigger size
Than ever the boy had seen them, and the lamplight
Was like a fire deep inside their eyes.

And there was something moving in between them,
Between their fiery hands in all that glow,
It made the sounds that woke him from his sleeping,
Like little sleigh bells ringing without snow.

It was birds they had, he saw two woolly
Heads with eyes like blueberries on soft brown,
And they were friends with father and his mother
And climbed into their hands and nestled down.

The birds talked low to them, and they were happy,
Being up so late here in the night,
And not afraid at all because his parents
Held them, and because there was the light.

The boy wished he was out there with the goslings
And in the middle of the happiness.
It was too much to ask. He closed his eyelids.
The sun was up, he sprang out quick to dress.

COAST HOUSES

It is fair, but this wind is the south,
The south wind carries sorrow in its mouth,
And people of the coast mind wind that grieves
Around their houses' corners and the eaves.

Maybe it is because houses are square
On the coast that south winds grieve so there
And hang a ghostly sadness on broad day
Like songs that men sang once but put away.

The people in the houses now have no
Need to heed the coast winds how they blow,
They have no men upon the sea to lie
At mercy of a changing wind and sky.

The houses, though, are older, and they may
Have power like a memory some way
To keep the ancient rituals of sorrow
And warn themselves of emptiness tomorrow.

They are in league with winds somehow and make
New hearts inside their walls slow up and ache,
They remind land people solemnly
Of death and beauty sometimes called the sea.

LAW BROKEN IN THE WOODS

Because I was so still and grown to be
Part of the woods, the bright thrush looked at me,
This round eye, then that, and friendly fear,
That kept the quick blood in him running clear,
Took her eyes from him. And something came
Too stealthy, silent, fast to have a name,
And where the thrush had been the bare branch swung,
Three feathers only on the false breeze hung,
One set of songs was over with and done.

And I was sorry I had broken one
Eternal law all beasts and birds obey:
I had been friendly, and fear took away
Her hand that trembles always on the heart
Of her wild children. So the bitter dart
Had flown, the chain of evening song was broken.
I was sad that tenderness had spoken
So in my eyes and my love so laid bare
The bird's breast to the death that rides the air.

THE NAME

When she had moved to town and left her house,
Frost came in and frightened out the mouse,
Leaned against the cellar till the stones
Fell in, and soft rain broke the bones
Of the roof, the wind pushed in the panes,
The swallows came in on their airy lanes
And raised their young where her own young had been,
Her house was lost to laughter and to men.

But out among homecoming firs and pines
The farmer-wife's narcissus kept its lines
Unbroken in wild grass that tried to hide it,
It kept its circle, did not let inside it
Any green with wildness in its blood,
Every May, there was a shining flood
Of tame beauty, white as ocean foam,
To show the farmyard here was still a home.

That constellation stood ringed round with spears,
Defiant of the ruin which the years
Had sent upon the farm, the golden eyes
All turned outward on their enemies.
She who had planted these seeds of the light
Would never go down nameless in the night,
For she had written here on time her name
In letters made of cool and living flame.

REUNION

A light came out of the slender boy's brown face,
He was alone and in a secret place
He never went to when the rest were by,
A little isle alone with sea and sky.

He had waded to it with his slim
Bare legs and that deep radiance on him
Which made him graceful as a thing born wild
And not a stout and tame man's handsome child.

He heard a sound, he turned as light as down
And stared a year-old deer straight in his brown
Face and felt his eyes expand in size;
They looked each other in their startled eyes.

The deer's slim ears were wide as they could be,
His legs were four sharp arrows dipped in sea,
Ready for flight, his nostrils drank the air,
But something kept the young deer rooted there.

It was not fear, he knew he faced as young
A creature as himself, some rhythm sung
Into his being from his life's quick start,
Some likeness kept him there with pounding heart.

The boy was not afraid, he knew he faced
A young thing through whose veins a beauty raced
Like his own and made his ribwork press;
His eyes were brimming full of tenderness.

And then the sound of dogs brought in the fear,
The arrows leapt to flight beneath the deer,
And he was gone in foaming waves, his tail
Bobbing white as he went off full sail.

The spell was broken, and the boy could smile
Like a boy again. But a long while
He felt beneath his smiling something deep
And beautiful as birds that fly through sleep.

TIDES

One thing he took great pride in, not a day
But what at any hour the man could say
Just how the tide was : dead low or turn or flood.
It was four hundred miles to the ocean, but his blood
Had the tides still in it. They still ran
Young as ever though he was an old man
And never would depend on time or tide
To change him any way before he died.

He had left off mentioning to his wife
About the time of tide, but it was life
To know it, the only young part to him;
He never talked to anyone who knew him
Of the mighty arms that reached and found him
And would not let him go but held around him
Like something he recalled when very young
Of arms around him and a low song sung.

The vast sea rose there, barred a diamond-white,
The moon wove at it high across the night,
His life was part of that unearthly web.
Men do not die except upon the ebb,
They used to say, back there beside the ocean.
He was safe as long as that slow motion
Lifted him up against the law of earth
As he was lifted in the hour of birth.

THRUSH WOODS

I know the place where there is always quiet,
The white-pine needles carpet all the ground,
A road winds on into a world-wide stillness,
And the thrushes sing the day around;
The thrushes do not wait for evening's coolness,
One blows his flute beneath the noonday sun,
Tries his lowest tune, his middle, highest,
And other thrushes answer one by one.

The road has nowhere but a single dwelling
To go to, and a quiet man lives there,
His children are men grown and grown-up women,
And they have gone and left the pasture bare.
Time does not go that roadway any longer,
The thrushes' timeless chorals climb and climb,
They sing as if it were forever Summer
And dew were always there and sunset time.

WHAT HAVE YOU DONE TO YOUR DAUGHTER?

"Miss Jinny,
What have you done to your beautiful daughter Anne?"

Dr. Lake was a happy-family man.
He believed in happiness, he believed
In families, his blonde small wife conceived
As regularly as the Spring swelled at its girdle.
On every path there was a cart to hurdle
Or a boy bent over and thick through
The arrogance of his small thighs, and new
Babies going on all fours. There were
No silences in his house. The stir
Of lusty playing, eating, sleeping, breeding
Went on all the time, gay and unheeding.
His house was like the south side of a hill
That May has warmed and made the rabbits spill
Over into clouds of tufts of brown
And each tuft with new eyes among the down.

"What have you done with your beautiful daughter Anne,
Miss Jinny?"

Dr. James Lake was a man
A planet away from this small being in bed,
Bright-eyed as a nestling left unfed.
Mrs. Virginia Barkesdale was a creature
Made beautiful with pain in every feature,
Arthritis and a studied and sad pride
Had made a steady flame of her inside,
And the flame came through her everywhere
And gathered like a nimbus on her hair.

[70]

She had lived six years propped on a pillow,
She had lived two hundred since the willow
Outside her window caught last evening's light,
She had lived two centuries in one night.
She had seen her daughter join the race
Who built this house, and slip over her young face
The mask which faces silence with deep eyes
And never changes line because of wise,
Tremendous matters going on behind
Its surface in what once has been a mind
But now is a universe where vast things race
Outside the day and night in dizzy space.
She had seen her daughter go insane,
Go up to join the two close to the rain
Under the mansion's eaves in locked-up rooms.
There the long sunbeams were the same as glooms,
And two fine-featured men sat erect and nice,
Tapping their fingers delicate and precise.
Their eyes were bright and luminous in their stare,
But servants could not tell what went on there
Behind the eyes, and servants left the food,
Too awed by their beauty to be rude.

"What have you done to your beautiful daughter, then?"

Mrs. Barkesdale saw Anne pass again, again
Outside her door, the livelong night of waking.
She saw Anne with the letters she was taking
One after one, as she had finished each, downstairs.
It was too late at night, and life, for prayers.
Mrs. Barkesdale said none, did not raise a hand.
The house was too big for one family to command,

Too big for years going faster by all clocks,
Rushing past hedges and slow-growing box.
Miss Jinny had done all that a mother could do,
Had sent Anne off to college and to new
Places far from seeds that carry death
A family in one place long sow each breath.

But Anne had found the one door to creep through
Back into her family and the house she knew.
She found the door of love that burns in vain.
She loved in silence. She was home again.
She wrote the man a letter now at last.
She wrote the man another. She wrote fast,
For the time was short. The cocks were crowing,
Magnolia petals on the lawn were snowing
Under the wind that brings the morning star.

Knowing you for the honorable man you are,
I must insist that you not much consider
My feelings. The edge of silence almost hid her,
She must write fast, there'd be long time for rest.
I am most sorry that I have confessed
A passion— No, that was not the word.
She heard the morning's earliest, smallest bird
Twitter in the willow overhead.
Someone moved in the rooms she'd learned to dread,
She must be quick. *—a sentiment not shared.*
I would have given much, could I have spared
Your feelings in this matter. There, her name.
She closed the letter quickly on her shame,
Rose, and took her candle to the landing.
The faithful Linda Lou was still there standing,

Standing as she had stood for sixteen years.
It was natural there should be tears
In Linda's eyes. She knew that letters might
Be cause of tears, written so late at night.
Linda took the letter in her hand,
And went downstairs and put it on the stand
Beside the others.

> People were very kind.
But there was another letter in Anne's mind.
She must make haste to write it. . . . She returned
To her room. She saw how the candle burned
Paler, and the window to the east
Was squares of gray, not black. Her dress was creased,
Her party dress. A dress does not last out
A night. Somehow she thought and thought about
The whole thing as a party. . . . There should be
Music. There was music in the tree,
The tree was full of birds, sharp-crying birds,
She could hardly wedge her letter's little words
Between the cries of birds. They filled the room,
They crowded out the candlelight and gloom.
Keen, sharp, they had an edge on them. She saw
They had cut her fingers. There was a flaw
On every finger. Her fingers had to stop,
Each one had a red and growing drop,
They dropped upon her letter. People should
Keep birds out of their houses. Now there would
Be trouble. The door upstairs had come
Unfastened. The birds! the blood, the hum
Of a thousand little voices she had never
Guessed had been there talking round her, ever.

The birds had pecked a hole down through the world!
She could see the cloud below her, curled,
And she stepped forward gladly. . . . This white, this
Cloud was lovely. Lost. Alone. Then the abyss.

Mrs. Virginia Barkesdale saw the beauty
Of the low, young sun, and now her duty
Was done. The sun was a steady candle
Set on the edge of earth. Her hands would handle
Each other this way a year, or two or three.
What did it matter how long it would be?
Her hands would clasp and unclasp many dawns,
And there would be robins teetering on the lawns
With their shadows long upon the dew.
There was plenty room up yonder there, she knew.
The family was one of the upstairs kind,
Old families often were. She did not mind
Any more. Anne wore her party frock,
At least, when she went up. Why did Lake talk
And talk and ask the same thing over so?
He should ask others if he wished to know
Who was responsible for Anne's ascent
To the upper chamber. She had spent
Enough breath as it was. He should go seek
His answer elsewhere. Let the others speak.

Ask of the trees, Dr. Lake, come up too near
My husband's house by year and year and year,
Wild trees too full of mocking-birds and song.
Ask the great trees, Dr. Lake, standing too long,
The trees as vast as ancient dinosaurs,
Some prone and dying, with stark, open claws.

Ask the three thousand acres of rich land,
Too much for one family to keep in hand,
Too wide a farm, these years, for one lord,
A weight to break a back however broad.
Too many rows to sow for a few fingers,
Once slaves are gone and only master lingers,
Too many crops, too few mouths to feed—
A thousand acres taken by the weed—
Too much to hold, and nothing much to sell,
Selling things will keep a family well.
Go ask the ancient family confidence
Why it saddled sons with an immense
Estate they could not sell and so escape
Into safe, careless living and the shape
Of varied days and living here and there
And coming upon fresh women fit to bear
Sons with safe ancestors on the mother's side,
Who had found life a walk and not a ride,
Safe ancestors in the smallest houses
To thicken blood diluted by carouses,
Small houses to offset the one great mansion
With Greek columns and a polished stanchion
To keep the gentleman all safe upstairs,
Once he had sown wild oats and proper heirs
And drunk and ridden hard and lived the code
Hard on the wife and on the horse he rode.

Go ask the code, the code's the thing to blame
For making men with narrow hips no tame
Loveliness can win but only coarse
Or fragile things, for making men who are worse
And splendider than stallions, with legs alive
To horseflesh, choosing angels when they wive,

Stay-in, shut-in women, sweet of breath,
And full of moonlight and the moths of death.
Go blame the sun. Go blame the sun-drowned South
Who always has death's flower in her mouth!

Go ask the trees, Dr. Lake, the luxuriant trees,
Drugged with long Summers of three centuries,
Drugged with the mocking-birds and mourning-doves,
Clogged with the honey of repeated loves.
Go ask the trees of the too-easy flowers,
Camellias and magnolias spilling showers
Of warm snow on the grass until the hours
Of Spring are hours lived inside of dreams.
Go ask the honeysuckle where it teems
And covers half the world, and myrtle rankles
And spreads sky-flakes as high as walkers' ankles.
Go ask the jasmine what it did to Anne,
But never ask the question of a man.
The jasmine is to blame, the flower of fire,
The honeysuckle wove the snare its wire.
Go ask the fireflies like fallen stars
And cows with udders dripping at the bars.
Go ask a dream. Go ask a soil too rich
For all but saints and wantons or a witch.
Go ask your questions, Doctor, of the sun,
It is, you know, a high and lecherous one.

Go ask this big house of too many rooms
And painted ancestors peering through its glooms.
Go ask the wardrobe opening its own doors.
Go ask the steps that come and go on floors
When no one's there. Go ask the painted lady
Too near the harp upstairs there, maybe,

And maybe it is her hands strum the strings
She used to play before her life took wings.
The portraits are to blame. Too many bright
Eyes there too proud to keep the common light
In them always, and so they changed and deepened
Rather than see their lonely passions cheapened
By long faithfulness to living within reason,
And so their owners went upstairs in season.

"Do not ask questions, Dr. Lake, of me.
Go back to your children and be free,
Go back to your breeding. I have years
Ahead of me in this house. There are no tears
For me to shed. Tears are for your kind,
Tears are for little houses.

                        "See, the blind
Has roses on it blossomed new today!
Be sure you shut the gate upon your way."

THE POOL

Though it was wild, the place was tended,
All at once the fir trees ended
And left a sunny place all grass,
The grass stayed short, and it let pass
A stream of water, thin as thread
And bright as beads. The stream was fed
From some mystery underground,
It fell like bells of smallest sound
Into a pool so clear it was
Deep as the tree-tops, though the moss
Waded in it at its deepest,
Where its banks curved down the steepest
The small white violets leaned and saw
Their faces reflected without flaw.

The air above was all blue eyes
And wings of burning dragonflies
Flying so fast they did not seem
More than the blue light of a dream.
A single cow's hoof could have made
A ruin of this careful glade.
But never a thirsty cow would dare
To drink such water clear as air
Or crop such violets, all white honey,
No frog would dare to cloud this sunny
Sea so solemnly dedicated
To life so delicate it weighted
The earth's lap with no heavier thigh
Than that on Spring's first butterfly.

CAT ON THE TABLE

My small cat upon my table
Treads as light as he is able,
He walks among my written words
As if he crept up on quick birds.

He puts down quicksilver feet
Without rustling any sheet,
It might be a mouse he stalks,
So cautiously the creature walks.

I am very proud to see
The opinion that he has of me,
He makes me think the words I write
May have some quality of flight.

Maybe my poems have a stir
Like that beneath a rabbit's fur,
Maybe now my cat can sense
Some live thing here, and so goes tense.

THE ISLAND MAN

He owned an island, that set him apart
From Monday's men who went the Monday ways.
He could be alone, and that was something
Other men had missed without once knowing
They missed the thing at all. It was like Sunday
With him all the week, great quiet leaned
Upon him like the slanting beams of the sun.
Birds knew it. They came closer day by day,
They looked him in the eyes and found him quiet,
They did not mind him being there, the rocks
Were not more harmless or more right than he.

He lay in bed at night and knew how his
Rocky island slanted under sea
And went deep down where men could never go,
Or day or night, or even wind and rain,
The cool fish swam around his part of earth
Like stars around the world deep in cool space,
They kept him separate, they kept the words
Which trouble life away from what he thought.
He thought without the words, without the pains
Of trying to put his feelings into sounds.
That was a fine thing : he could see his thoughts
Go past him like the waves that kept him safe.

HOW TO MAKE THE COW GIVE DOWN

To make the cow give down her milk
A man must lean against the silk
Where her leg-bone meets the round
Of her belly, with unfrowned
Forehead, and the thoughts behind
His warm brow should be the kind
Which make him feel how good are ones
Who turn the corn ears into sons.
Men start with lonely, silent earth
Under their thighs and bring to birth
Children out of the earth they turn
And cows coming home when sunsets burn
Lower and lower and let the stars
Shine through when a man lets down the bars
To his cows and sees his children leap
Like young calves at the gates of sleep.

A man must make music with his hands,
Grip the udder with bands on bands,
Downward, the direction of all life,
Be it to calf or child or wife,
Away from the giver to the given,
The motion by which dead space is riven
By living streams of starry light.
A man must make his hunger as right
To the cow as her calves do,
Make lips of his fingers, draw milk through,
He must make music underneath
The creature, make each hand a sheath.

[81]

He must make no sudden motion
But be relentless as the ocean,
Firm and fierce and tenderer than
Anything on earth but man.

HE KNEW HIS WAY

He had never been inside this house,
And it was night, but still he knew his way.
Here was the place for the hearth to be, and here
The door should be, and here a window frame,
And, sure enough, the solid wall let through
Twelve dim rectangles dusted with the stars.
By rights the stairs were there, and there they were,
Making a long road up to taking rest,
Making a short road up to making love.

He knew his way because this was New England,
And this house was an old one. All his roots
Had followed out these lines three hundred years,
They knew the places where men put their tap-roots
Upon the hearth and round the pantry-walls,
Dim ancestors of his below the earth-light,
Six feet down, put out his hands for him,
He did not need his eyes, the eyeless sires
Who shaped the contours of his skull and thighs
Led him straight without the use of sight.
The house was one built right, and he belonged here,
Here was the door that led up to the chamber
Where his father begot him, here the door
That led into the room where he would die.

BOY ON A STUMP

The town boy playing skip and jump
Could not resist the maple stump
Higher than his shining head,
He embraced it, and he spread
His thighs far round as they would go.
He worked his knees and went up slow,
Worked his elbows, belly, heart,
His seams all threatening to part,
He tautened up with strength, his pride
Bulged his breeches out back side,
He drew a deep draught from his soul,
And stretched out face-down on his goal.

He righted up and stood profound
Higher up above the ground
Than he would be again in life
When he walked out with a wife
And had a boy with itching knees
Wanting to climb up all the trees.
He drank in more things in his view
Than confident and tall men do.
This was a top to things, this look,
Every deep breath that he took
Made him in his body's span
So much less boy, so much more man.

THE ALMANAC

The Bible was one center of the farm,
But it was in the parlor and the cold
Five months of the year. There man set down
Births of his young and death dates of his old.
It was too large and thick a book to hold.

There was a better center to his days
In the kitchen, back of the kitchen range,
The little paper book hung on a nail
That told him when the moon and tides would change.
The Zodiac beasts marched through it, stout and strange.

The pages always had the pleasant heat
Of beech or birch wood keeping kettles hot,
The book was just the size of a farmer's hand,
Its pages felt good as the reader thought,
The farmer reading smelt the savory pot.

The little book was bigger than it seemed,
It had the silver flood and ebb of tides,
The twenty-four white horses of the winds,
And times for bridegrooms and the times of brides,
It held the seeds that swell the earth's green sides.

It told the farmer when to sow his oats
And how to oil the harness of his span,
It told him when the stars bent down to light
Him to the bed and beauty of a man,
It told him when the Ram and Lion ran.

PINES AFTER SNOW

No man knows the handsomeness of pines
Till they stand slimmer under weight of snow,
In silence, under cover of the night,
Great presences have marched up row on row.

A householder looks out through common panes
And sees a tall white stranger by his fence,
His airy hands made thick and powerful,
Wrapped in wildness, spotless and immense.

Half of the earth has climbed up on the skies,
No bird dares light, no shaking rabbit stir,
The world stands silent and holds in its breath
Before strong gods wrapped lonely in their fur.

LATE-WINTER EVENING

The day was getting bleak and old,
The pine trees hugged up with the cold,
Snow was sending out blue light
And growing harder for the night.
Far away an axe that chopped
Double with its echo stopped.
The single watcher in the wood
Hardly breathed and stood and stood,
Something was coming a good clip—
Tat-tattoo and *lippety-lip*.
It was a rabbit. Each end went
Up and down, and then the scent
Of the alien struck him hot,
The rabbit flattened ears and squat
In his latest triple track,
Froze, and his globed eyes burned black.
Five feet away he suffered till
His fear burned out, he bobbed uphill.
The watcher went the other way,
The beach spread dead white down the bay,
The sea beyond was dark as soot,
This watcher stopped there with one foot
Ahead of the other. There could not be
Much more to the day to see.
Somewhere in the gathering dusk
Wild ducks were talking, and the husk
Of some Summer thing gave hollow
Warning that a wind would follow.

I HEARD SPRING

I heard Spring a thousand miles away
In the thin end of a Winter night,
It came and found me in the midst of dreams
With only starlit icicles for light.

It spoke to me in sleep, I heard it plain,
It said three words, but those three words were law.
I woke up smiling, for I knew I had
Heard a crow sing out his *caw, caw, caw.*

The bird had kept his sharp tongue in his head
Long months, but it stabbed like a sword blade now,
And violets would soon smoke up the woods
And crows and bluets march beside the plow.

IT TAKES A BOY

It is good to see a single plowman,
But it is better when the man is two
And has his son beside him driving,
Or holding, and the two go side by side.
Soil knows its master when it sees its master
Has sown good seed to show the land the way.
And a boy is closer than his father
To what is under plows—which is plain life;
His two bare feet touch on the trembling thing,
And it comes up his warm legs as the sap
Comes up young trees in Spring of the young year.
A man alone cannot work half the magic
Of multiplying corn, it takes a boy,
It takes a boy who is not half through budding,
And wherever he sets his bare brown feet
Young corn will find encouragement to grow,
Growing things like growing things beside them;
Maybe they mix a pollen dust, these two,
A good farm is a farm that blossoms boys.

RACCOON HUNT

The boy still small enough to be kissed
Walks a wild world of silver mist,
The tame men he is following there
Breathe out wings each side their hair,
Their lanterns stab out starry holes
In the night, and aureoles
Wheel around them as they swing.
Far off, the hounds the boy knew sing
Like demons from the moon's dark side,
And the echoes roll out wide.

Now the thing with needle nose
That dredges ponds with silver toes
For his supper leaves the world
And at the tree-top trembles curled
Around a branch. His beads of eyes
Catch the lanterns, grow in size,
Catch afire with deep hate
At the snuffling and the great
Animals that nose his tree
Among false stars that wander free.

The boy who should have been abed
Hears the stab and sees the red
Fire reach straight to its mark.
Down comes the dainty and the dark
Creature beautiful and lost,
Creature with the rings like frost
Scrolled around his tail, and lies
In the lantern light and dies.
And the boy is first to stroke
The wildness ebbing from his cloak.

[90]

JUG BELOW THE STARS

He never could be sure what was behind it,
Dreams ought to warn one—if it was a dream,
It was the way dreams are, clear as a crystal,
And while he still was in it, he could hear
How he was telling himself it was a dream.
But nothing ever came of what went on there
That night, as far as he could ever tell,
And that was why the thing haunted him so.

He had just landed home, it was October,
And stars were out in millions on the bay,
He had his lantern low to watch his footing,
And so came close enough to touch the man.
It gave him quite a start, it was past midnight
And all good island folks were safe abed,
No one had business out, this was a stranger.
He saw his legs before he saw his head,
The stranger had a jug with flowers on it.
"There used to be a spring of water here,"
The words were not so loud as one would look for
From a man so close, but they were clear,
"I wonder, could you tell me where the spring is?"
He pointed out the place, he did not say
A single word, he afterwards remembered.
The stranger seeking water turned his face
And walked that way. The man could not recall
Anything of the face. His light was low,
Maybe that was why. He heard the sounds
Of the bubbling jug, he did not move,
He never moved a muscle. Then the odd
Night prowler went upon his lonely way.

He knew that, though he did not hear him going—
And that was queer, no footfalls on the stones!
And then it struck him that the night was cold,
Very cold and full of strange high light.
And something more, the shoes his lantern lighted,
It came over him, had had wide buckles,
All the legs were stockings to the knee,
And the hat had made a dark three-cornered
Patch upon the starry top of night.
He came to with a start, ran up the ledges,
There was no sign of anyone at all,
There was no boat, no ship against the starlight—
It would have been a tall one for those shoes!
As he went home, he heard the first cock crow.

Nothing ever came of what he saw there,
But he would hear the flowered jug drink water
Under the starlight till his dying day,
And his common cove and the bare island,
From that night on, seemed somehow high and strange
And the bayberry powdered with a dust of stars.

ALL THE LIVING GIVE THANKS

We see the Spring come steady on,
The maples bleeding leaves, wet flowers,
Hepaticas, and bluets come
Behind them only fourteen hours,
And watch wild-cherry walk the woods
Upon rhodora's heel,
And always, always ruin 1ast
Upon the living steal,
We see the lights of anemones
Go out and new lamps come
Hung on the dogtooth violets,
And hear the first bees' hum
Pile up to thunderheads of sound
Above the dusky clover,
See white waves of daisies roll
Up hills and always cover over
The flowers of the Spring, and hear
Golden thunder rattle
And see the goldenrod go up
The pasture past the cattle,
And watch the frostflowers hurrying past
Ahead of blooms of frost,
Bright boys so different each from each
Into the men gone on and lost,
Wide-handed men so sure of strength,
The lovers seeming new
Constellations and new moons
Betrayed, see all men sinking through
The solid earth beside their friends,
And never a hand to reach them aid,

And children fall out among the stars
Before half of their games are played,
And newer men crowd older men
With Winter on their hair
Off the green world among bare stars,
And star by star extinguished there,
And always, always the swift shade
Behind each running day
And the wise noses of the hounds
On every track the hare has made,
The eyes of lynxes and of doves
Burning out alway,
See sweet principalities
Of bees consume the Summer saved,
And see the grain of bitter snow
Where the sweet green corn leaves waved!

And great thanks we the living give
To watch the ruin come, and live.

FAR TREES KEEP UP

I can still remember it all:
How far great pines when I was small
Kept pace as I and my father rode
Although the near trees backward flowed,
The great pines coming, the small going back,
I looked at the tall trees till my back
Felt like a tree, I looked so long,
And somehow the sight was like a song.

Far things are keeping up with me still:
The stars go with me over the hill,
The moon keeps step with me. Though he
Who drove through Spring and Summer with me
Is gone from sight, there is my son,
He sits by a father as I sat by one;
Fathers outlast a single face,
And sons come on an endless pace.

Love lasts longer than one man,
Pride marches beyond one family's span,
Pity lasts longer than one mother,
Longer than one unhappy brother.
Men will never outdistance joy
Or the worship of a boy,
Sorrow will catch them one dark day,
Grief goes beside us all the way.

My son's eyes turn up to mine,
He has noticed how a pine,
Far away, is keeping beside
Us two old friends upon our ride.

His eyes are brighter than new bees,
Discovering how the distant trees
Keep up, while near ones backward flow.
His eyes are my eyes long ago.

DEFINITION FOR A POEM

Listen then, and learn from this
What thing they call a poem is:

It is a small thing shut away
From wide reason and broad day.
It is a woman crowding wood
Into a cookstove in the good
Smell of run-over apple juice,
A sharp point to a year, a noose
Slipped on a lawless moment's rush,
An old man's lying in the hush
Of his lonely house in bed,
Practicing at being dead
A month before his time for dying
And hearing silence come, and sighing.
A poem is a girl who shells
New green peas and hears the bells
In her lover's blood peal out
As his arms close her about.
A poem is a wind-lit spark,
Two boys whispering in a dark
Haymow secrets to each other
Never whispered to a brother,
A blazing rooster as he treads
His wing before a hen and spreads
Fire everywhere he touches.
A poem is the act that clutches
On a sudden lovely thing
Like falcons on a sparrow's wing,

[97]

Cruel, most compact, unblind,
Changing a muscle to a mind,
An act too beautiful for space
Like dewdrops on a cobweb's lace.

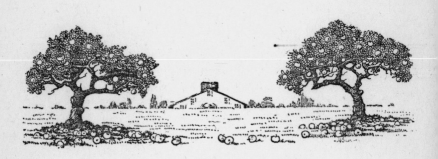

A